ALEXANDER THE GREAT

Peggy Pancella

Heinemann Library
Chicago, Illinois

Customer Service 888-454-2279
Visit our website at www.heinemannlibrary.com

Designed by Lisa Buckley
Maps by John Fleck
Photo research by Julie Laffin
Printed and Bound in the United States by Lake Book Manufacturing, Inc.

08 07 06 05 04
10 9 8 7 6 5 4 3 2 1

Library of Congress Cataloging-in-Publication Data
Pancella, Peggy
    Alexander the Great / Peggy Pancella.
        p. cm. -- (Historical biographies)
Summary: Presents an overview of Alexander the Great's life as well as his influence on history and the world.
Includes bibliographical references and index.
    ISBN 1-4034-3699-1 (HC) -- ISBN 1-4034-3707-6 (pbk.)
  1. Alexander, the Great, 356-323 B.C.--Juvenile literature. 2. Greece--History--Macedonian Expansion, 359-323 B.C.--Juvenile literature. 3. Generals--Greece--Biography--Juvenile literature. 4. Greece--Kings and rulers--Biography--Juvenile literature. [1. Alexander, the Great, 356-323 B.C. 2. Kings, queens, rulers, etc. 3. Generals. 4. Greece--History--Macedonian Expansion, 359-323 B.C.] I. Title. II. Series.
    DF234.P29 2003
    938'.07'092--dc21
                                       2003005891

Acknowledgments
The author and publisher are grateful to the following for permission to reproduce copyright material: Icon, p. 22 North Wind Picture Archives; pp. 4, 8, 12, 16 , 21, 27 Ancient Art & Architecture Collection LTD; p. 6 Giraudon/ Art Resource; p. 7 Alinari/Art Resource, NY; pp. 9, 17, 20, 26 Réunion des Musées Nationaux/Art Resource, NY; p. 10 Nimatallah/Art Resource, NY; p. 11 Scala/Art Resource; pp. 13, 24 Mary Evans Picture Library; pp. 14, 15, 28 Erich Lessing/Art Resource, NY; p. 18 Roger Wood/Corbis; pp. 19, 23, 29 The Granger Collection

Cover photograph: The Art Archive

Special thanks to Michelle Rimsa for her comments in preparation of this book.

Some words are shown in bold, **like this.** You can find out what they mean by looking in the glossary.

Many names and terms may be found in the pronunciation guide.

The cover of this book shows a statue of Alexander the Great. It is a copy of a statue that was made in 338 B.C.E. by a Greek artist. The icon seen throughout this book shows another statue of Alexander.

Contents

Who Was Alexander the Great?

Alexander the Great lived more than 2,000 years ago in Macedonia, a land to the north of Greece. He became king of Macedonia when he was only twenty years old. Alexander was also a mighty soldier. He conquered many lands throughout the **Middle East.**

The world in Alexander's time

During Alexander's lifetime, many countries struggled for power. Rulers fought battles with other countries. The winner could take over the other country and add it to his **empire.**

Macedonia was near Greece, a part of the world where great changes were happening. The Greeks were making many new discoveries. Art, science, and **literature** were developing quickly. Most countries were ruled by kings, but Greece was not. Instead, the country was made up of **city-states.** Each city-state had its own government.

In Macedonia, however, most people were poor and hardworking. Macedonia's ruler was a king who kept all the power for himself.

▶ Alexander opened new trade **routes.** He spread the Greek language and culture to distant lands. This statue of Alexander can be seen in the Glyptotek museum in the country of Denmark.

▶ Macedonia began as a small area in northern Greece. As the kingdom gained power, it grew to include parts of present-day Albania, Bulgaria, and the country that is still known as Macedonia.

How do we know about Alexander the Great?

Although Alexander lived a long time ago, many writings about him survive. It was probably **customary** in Macedonia to keep a record of everything a king did. In addition, many friends, relatives, soldiers, and others wrote about Alexander. **Archaeologists** have studied some of the places that Alexander visited. They have found **artifacts** that tell more about Alexander and his life.

Key dates

356 B.C.E.	Birth of Alexander
336 B.C.E.	Alexander becomes king of Macedonia
332 B.C.E.	Alexander becomes **pharaoh** of Egypt
330 B.C.E.	Alexander becomes Great King of Persia
323 B.C.E.	Death of Alexander

Watch the dates

B.C.E. after a year date means "before the common era." This is used instead of the older abbreviation B.C. The years are counted backwards toward zero. **Historians** are not sure about some dates of Alexander's life. You may see different dates in different books.

A Ruler's Son

Alexander was born in 356 B.C.E. His father was King Philip II of Macedonia, and his mother was named Olympias. This royal family lived in Pella, the capital city of Macedonia.

Alexander's parents

King Philip II had come to power in 359 B.C.E. Philip was a strong fighter who won many battles. He used his power to unite the Macedonians into a strong fighting force. He then attacked the Greek **city-states.** Each city-state alone was not large or strong enough to defeat Philip's army. And the city-states did not help one another fight back. One by one, the city-states **surrendered.** Philip controlled most of Greece.

◄ This statue of Philip II was found in a **tomb** in Greece. The coin below from the 300s B.C.E. also shows what Philip II might have looked like.

Alexander's mother, Olympias, was also a strong person. Philip was often away from home, so Olympias usually took care of Alexander. As a result, she became very close to her son.

The young Alexander

With parents like these, it is not surprising that Alexander grew up to be brave and sure of himself. He was also very headstrong. He did not like to change his mind, even if what he planned sometimes seemed to be impossible.

▲ The statue above shows Alexander on his horse, Bucephalus.

When Alexander was about ten years old, his father took him to a fair. They saw a beautiful horse that Philip was interested in buying, but the horse would not let anyone come near it. Alexander told his father that he could tame the horse. He had noticed that the horse was afraid of its shadow. When Alexander turned the horse toward the sun, he was able to ride around on it. This horse, Bucephalus, later carried Alexander to many adventures.

Alexander and travelers

Guests often visited Philip's palace, and Alexander was taught to take care of their needs. When he was a boy, some men from Persia came to visit. Philip was not home, but young Alexander welcomed the travelers. He asked questions about their trip and their homeland. Such talks may have gotten Alexander interested in traveling to other parts of the world.

Life in Macedonia

During Alexander's time, Macedonia was divided into two regions: Upper Macedonia and Lower Macedonia. Several **tribes** lived in Upper Macedonia. The people spoke their own languages, but not Greek. In Lower Macedonia, near Pella, most people spoke Greek and followed the Greek way of life. Philip—and later Alexander—had a hard job uniting these very different areas.

Work in Macedonia

Most people in Macedonia were poor farmers. They raised food to eat and trade. One of their most valuable crops was olives. Olives could be eaten plain. They could also be crushed to make oil for cooking or for burning in lamps. Other workers in Macedonia hunted animals or made crafts. Many other people were soldiers in Philip's army.

◄ This vase from ancient Greece shows workers gathering olives.

Daily living

Alexander's life was very different from the lives of most Macedonians. The royal family lived in a fine palace with many rooms. Families like his had plenty of meat, fish, and fine foods to eat. Their clothing was made from cotton and silk, and it was often dyed or beautifully decorated. The rich sometimes had servants. They often enjoyed playing games and watching actors, dancers, and musicians perform.

In contrast, most Macedonians lived much simpler lives. Their homes were built of mud brick and usually had just a few rooms. Their food was also plain— bread, wine, cheese, fruits, and vegetables. Poor families wore the same basic clothing as the rich, but their clothes were made of rougher cloth. These people did not usually have the money or the free time to watch entertainers.

▶ **A museum called the Louvre in Paris, France, has this statue of Alexander's head on display. The nose on the statue has been damaged.**

Getting an education

Not all children in Macedonia went to school. Children from poor families usually had to help work at home. Even among the rich, only boys usually went to school, starting around age seven. They learned to read, write, count, and even play music and sports. Girls usually stayed home and learned to spin, weave, and cook. These skills helped prepare them to have their own families.

Training for Success

Alexander knew that someday he would become king of Macedonia. He had to learn reading, writing, and other school subjects. He also needed to know how to be a good ruler.

Early tutoring

When Alexander was about seven years old, Philip hired a **tutor** named Leonidas for him. Leonidas thought Alexander's comfortable lifestyle was making him lazy and spoiled. He believed that hard work would help Alexander become strong. Each night, to make Alexander hungry for breakfast, Leonidas made the boy march a long way. Then, in the morning, he gave Alexander only a little food, so that he would be very hungry at dinnertime. Leonidas even searched Alexander's room for any food hidden there. Leonidas probably also taught Alexander battle skills, such as driving a **chariot** and using swords and spears.

Studying with a master

In 342 B.C.E., Philip invited the famous Greek **philosopher** Aristotle to Pella. Aristotle taught Alexander and some of Alexander's friends.

▲ This statue shows what Aristotle probably looked like.

The young men studied subjects such as **literature**, philosophy, and law. Alexander especially enjoyed science. Later, he took scientists along when his army traveled. They made maps and collected samples of plants and animals. They also kept detailed records of things they saw on their travels.

In their free time, the young men rode horses, practiced music, and went hunting. Alexander enjoyed these days very much. He respected Aristotle, and they stayed in touch for many years. Alexander also made lasting friendships. One friend, Hephaestion, became especially close. He went along on most of Alexander's later travels.

▲ This painting from the 1600s shows Alexander reading the *Iliad* in bed while a soldier guards him.

The Iliad

The *Iliad* is a long poem probably written in the 700s B.C.E. Its story tells about a war the Greeks fought. The Greeks attacked the city of Troy with the help of their leader and hero, Achilles. Alexander admired Achilles and wanted to be like him. He liked the *Iliad* so much that he memorized almost all of it. He even kept a copy of it under his pillow.

From Soldier to King

When Alexander turned sixteen, he stopped studying and joined the Macedonian army. His father had already defeated most of the Greek **city-states.** If Philip could defeat Athens and Thebes, he would control all of Greece. His troops would then be strong enough to attack the great Persian **empire** in Asia. The Greeks and Persians had been enemies for hundreds of years.

First taste of war

In 338 B.C.E., Alexander fought in a battle at Chaeronea, a town on Mount Petrachus in Greece. He and his horse, Bucephalus, led the **cavalry** against the Thebans. At the same time, Philip led the **infantry** against the Athenians. Soon, both city-states were defeated. The next year, Macedonia made an agreement with all the Greek city-states except Sparta. They promised to help one another fight when needed. And Philip became leader of their combined army.

▲ This gold coin shows Philip in battle.

Troubles at home

Now that Alexander and Philip were working together, they got along better than before. However, that changed when Philip fell in love with a young woman and decided to marry her. It was normal at the time for rulers to have many wives. However, Alexander and his mother did not like the new bride. A fight broke out at the wedding feast. Afterward, Alexander and Olympias moved away to avoid more trouble.

Alexander later returned to Pella, but the problems were not over. During a celebration in 336 B.C.E., Philip was killed by one of his own bodyguards. Some people guessed that Alexander or Olympias planned the murder because they were so upset with Philip. Others thought the Persians were responsible. In the end, it did not matter who had committed the murder. Philip was dead, and Alexander would take his place as king.

▶ This drawing of Olympias was created in about 360 B.C.E. by an unknown artist.

Demosthenes and Isocrates

During this time of change in Greece, many people offered different ideas about running the country. Demosthenes, an **orator** from Athens, wanted each city-state to make its own decisions. He thought Macedonia should leave Greece alone. Philip preferred the ideas of Isocrates. Isocrates taught that Greece would be strong if the city-states worked together. He also thought fighting Persia would make Greece stronger.

Leader of Macedonia

Alexander was only twenty years old when he became king of Macedonia. Some people thought he was too young to rule well. Others supported Alexander, including Philip's most powerful **generals** and the army.

Gaining peace at home

Before Alexander could fight the Persians, he had to handle other problems. Several Greek **city-states** were making trouble. Some **tribes** in northern Macedonia were also causing problems. All these enemies were testing the new king to see how strong he was. Alexander decided to fight the Greeks first. The Greeks were not ready to fight back, and he defeated them quickly. In Macedonia, the tribes fought much harder, but they finally **surrendered**.

Another test came when people in the southern city-state of Thebes **revolted.** Alexander burned down much of the city and sold many of the Thebans as slaves. After that, all the other city-states quit fighting.

▼ This map shows how large the Persian **empire** was. The Persian capital city, Persepolis, is marked with a star.

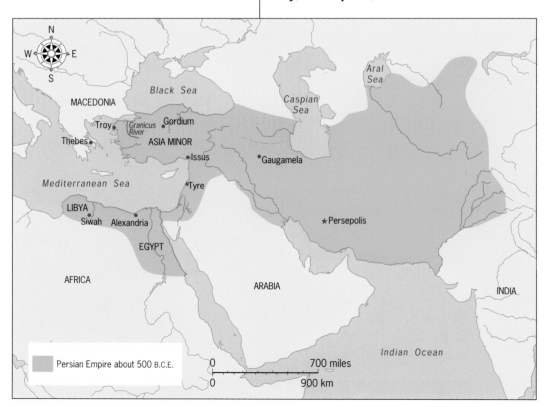

Persian Empire about 500 B.C.E.

0   700 miles
0   900 km

Into Asia Minor

In 334 B.C.E., Alexander felt ready to fight the Persians. He left part of his army at home to help keep peace. The rest of the soldiers headed east toward Asia Minor (now Turkey). Alexander brought more than 30,000 **infantry** and 5,000 **cavalry**. He also brought scientists, poets, and many others.

The army's first stop was the city of Troy. There, Alexander visited the **tomb** of the great warrior Achilles. He took a shield and other **armor** from the tomb to use for himself. Perhaps he hoped these items would bring him good luck.

Kindness and cruelty

Alexander usually treated his soldiers well. He shared his riches with them and gave them fine funerals when they died. Alexander also tried to show mercy to his enemies. If people surrendered without much fighting, he usually left them alone. This helped him earn their support. However, when enemies fought back, as the Thebans did, Alexander tried to destroy them.

Battles in Asia Minor

The Persian king, Darius III, was far away. He thought Alexander would be easy to defeat, so he did not hurry to meet him. He sent his **general** Memnon to lead the first attack against Alexander and his soldiers.

Early success

Memnon's soldiers met Alexander's soldiers at the Granicus River. Alexander's men had to cross the river to reach the enemy. At first, things did not go well, and Alexander was nearly killed. But the Persians were not ready for a long battle. The Greek army outlasted them.

▲ Alexander can be seen on his horse, Bucephalus, at the center of this painting. It shows the battle near the city of Issus.

Next, Alexander took over some nearby Persian lands. He also tried to take over many towns along the coast. Persia had a powerful navy, but the ships needed supplies. They could not get what they needed if Alexander controlled all the **ports.**

Alexander meets Darius

Meanwhile, Darius was coming closer. The two armies finally met near the city of Issus. The Persian soldiers shot many arrows at the Greeks. Then, Alexander ordered his men to charge straight at the shooters. This move surprised the Persians. The Persians kept fighting, but Darius and his men finally gave up and ran away.

Darius left behind his tents and many belongings. He also left his wife, mother, and two daughters behind. Alexander was kind to the women and treated them well. Darius wrote to Alexander, asking for his family's safe return. He offered to work together with Alexander. But Alexander refused. He wanted to rule Persia alone.

▼ This painting shows an artist's idea of what the battle between Darius and Alexander might have looked like.

The Gordian knot

In a city Alexander came upon during his travels, he saw a puzzle called the Gordian knot. This knot was made of rope, and it fastened two parts of a wagon. It was very tangled and seemed impossible to untie. Whoever could undo it was supposed to become ruler of all Asia. There are two stories about how Alexander undid the knot. He may have loosened it to make it easier to untie, or he may have simply cut it with his sword.

Gaining Power

Alexander continued taking over more **ports.** Some cities **surrendered** easily, but Tyre would not. One part of the city of Tyre was hard to attack because it was on an island that had high walls all around it. Alexander had his men build a causeway, or raised road, to the island.

Victory at Tyre

It took about seven months to complete the causeway. The people of Tyre tried everything they could think of to stop the workers. At last Alexander's men attacked. They rammed against Tyre's walls until they broke through. They killed thousands of people and took many more thousands as slaves.

After this happened, most of the Persian soldiers saw that the Greeks were more powerful. Darius wanted to end the fighting, too. He wrote to Alexander again, offering many rewards for his family's return. But again Alexander refused.

▼ **This photo shows the remains of an arena in the city of Tyre, which is in present-day Lebanon.**

18

Alexander the pharaoh

Alexander traveled south to Egypt, a very rich area of the Persian **empire**. Egyptians did not want to live under Persian rule any longer. They named Alexander their **pharaoh**, or ruler. In Egypt, Alexander **founded** a great city along the Mediterranean Sea. He named it Alexandria after himself. Alexandria quickly became a trading center. It had schools, museums, a zoo, and a library.

Alexander also went to Siwah, a desert **oasis** in what is now the country of Egypt. He visited an **oracle** of Amen, an important Egyptian god. Alexander went inside alone and asked questions privately. No one knows what he asked or what answers he received. Some people think Alexander was told that he was a god's son. After his visit to Siwah, he began to call himself the son of Amen and Zeus. Zeus was an important Greek god.

▲ This coin shows Alexander with the horns of a ram. The god Amen was often shown as a ram. The horns were meant to show that Alexander was the son of Amen.

Alexander the god

The Egyptians believed in many gods and built **temples** to worship them. They also thought that their pharaoh was like a god on earth. Therefore, they worshiped and respected him. In 1939, an Egyptian **archaeologist** found a temple in the desert. It had been built in honor of Alexander. Later, another smaller temple was discovered. Maybe the Egyptians really did treat Alexander as a god!

Great King of Persia

Darius was busy preparing for his next battle with Alexander. He had new weapons, including 200 **chariots** with sharp blades on their wheels. He also had more men—about five times as many as Alexander.

The battle of Gaugamela

In the fall of 331 B.C.E., Alexander reached Gaugamela, where Darius was waiting. Alexander's **advisers** thought he should attack at night to surprise the Persians. But Alexander did not want his own soldiers to be confused in the darkness. Instead, they waited until morning.

When the battle began, the Persian chariots attacked quickly. However, the Greek army moved to the sides. The Persian chariots rolled through the empty space in the middle. Meanwhile, the Greeks were losing on other parts of the battlefield. Then, Alexander saw an opening between the Persian soldiers.

▲ **This painting by French artist Jacques Courtois shows the battle of Gaugamela.**

Alexander charged through and aimed his spear at Darius. The spear missed, and Darius ran away again.

Chasing Darius

Alexander did not want Darius to escape this time. He followed the Persian leader across Asia. One of Alexander's first stops was the city of Babylon. The people there welcomed the Greeks and shared treasures with them. At Persepolis, the capital of Persia, Alexander took all the treasures he could find out of the royal palace.

▲ This photo shows the stairs that lead to the remains of Darius's palace in Persepolis.

After staying in Persepolis for about five months, he burned the palace down to show his power.

Alexander finally caught up with Darius in the desert near the Caspian Sea. Some of Darius's own men were holding him prisoner. They were ashamed of their leader's weakness. When Alexander came near, the men quickly stabbed Darius to death. Now Alexander alone ruled all of Persia.

Darius and Alexander

Darius and Alexander were from different places, but they had a lot in common. Both of them were strong leaders and fighters. They wanted to rule large areas of land. But Darius's army was no match for Alexander's. Darius probably did not like losing battles and having to beg for peace. Even his best offers were not good enough for Alexander.

Trouble in the Empire

Now that he was Great King of Persia, Alexander faced many challenges. One of his main problems was keeping both the Greeks and the Persians happy.

▲ This drawing shows what the wedding of Alexander and Roxane might have looked like.

Efforts at peace

Alexander tried hard to bring the people together. He began by creating one kind of money that everyone could use. This made trade much easier. Alexander also combined the two armies. He set up new governments in the lands he conquered. Persians were in charge of some things and Greeks were in charge of other things.

Alexander knew his troops were unhappy. They were tired of fighting and of being so far from home. Alexander held feasts and shared riches with the men. He also encouraged them to find Persian wives, so they would not get too homesick. Alexander chose a wife for himself, too— a Persian princess named Roxane.

Growing unrest

However, the men were not satisfied. They did not think Persian people should share power with Greek people. They also thought Alexander was acting too much like Persian people did. He wore Persian clothing, followed some Persian **customs**, and had Persian friends.

The men complained so much that it became hard for Alexander to trust them. When an important officer said too many bad things about him, Alexander had the man killed. Another old friend, Cleitus, spoke against Alexander at a party. Alexander became angry and lost control. He took a spear from a guard and stabbed Cleitus. After that happened, when his men disagreed with him, they kept quiet about it.

▲ The soldier shown in the drawing above, Philotas, was killed by Alexander. Alexander discovered that Philotas was planning to overthrow him.

Proskynesis

Alexander's men did not like the Persian custom called *proskynesis*. The Persians blew kisses to their rulers and bowed so low that their foreheads sometimes touched the ground. Alexander wanted everyone to bow to him as a sign of respect, but his soldiers refused to bow. They made fun of him. Alexander did not like it when his soldiers laughed at him. He soon stopped asking his soldiers to bow.

Moving Eastward

Even though they usually kept quiet about it, Alexander's men were more unhappy than ever. The weather was bad, and the land was very difficult to travel. Then, Alexander announced plans to conquer the rest of the world. He believed India was the last country he needed to defeat.

Preparing for battle

People in Alexander's time did not know much about the land or how far away other kingdoms really were. Alexander thought India was a small country near the edge of Asia. In fact, India was much bigger than Alexander guessed.

In 326 B.C.E., Alexander led his men across the Indus River to the city of Taxila. There, the troops prepared for battle. The conditions were difficult. The weather was very hot, and it also rained for days on end. Poisonous snakes were common in the area. Many soldiers were bitten, and some of them died.

Fighting against Porus

Finally, Alexander's army met King Porus at the Hydaspes River. Porus ruled an area near Taxila. He had more men than Alexander. He also had about 200 elephants. The elephants scared the Greeks and their horses.

▶ **Porus and his soldiers rode elephants into battle.**

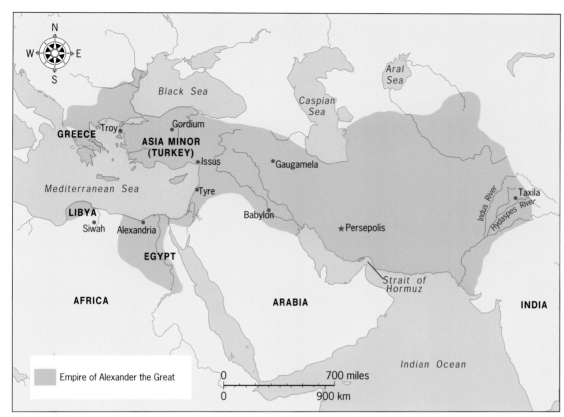

▼ This map shows how far Alexander's **empire** stretched across Asia.

Day after day, Alexander made it look as though he was going to lead his troops into battle. He had them gather at different places along the riverbank. On the other side, Porus moved his men and elephants to meet the Greeks. Porus finally decided that Alexander would never attack, so he stopped moving his troops.

That night, Alexander's men sneaked across the river far from Porus's camp. They surprised Porus and defeated his troops. Many men died in the fighting. Alexander's horse, Bucephalus, was hurt and later died. Unlike Darius, Porus did not run away when he lost. As a reward for his bravery, Alexander let him rule a large kingdom.

A Difficult Return

Alexander wanted to conquer the rest of India. However, his men were tired of rain, snakes, poor food, and difficult battles. They refused to go any farther. Alexander was very upset, but he had to give his men what they wanted. On the way home, he wanted to find a sea **route** to use for trade.

The travel was very difficult. Food, water, and other supplies ran low. Some of the land was rocky, and some was hot, dry desert.

▲ This painting from the 1600s shows Alexander entering Babylon in a golden **chariot.**

Many men, including Alexander, were hurt in battles along the way, and others died of sickness or lack of drinking water. It took them two months to reach the **Strait** of Hormuz, and about three-quarters of the men had died.

Problems in the empire

As Alexander traveled, he tried to restore order. Some government leaders had caused trouble while he was away. Alexander let many of his older soldiers retire. However, they complained when he hired young Persian soldiers instead. They did not like Persian soldiers to have so much power.

▲ This marble statue of Alexander shows an artist's vision of what Alexander looked like when he died.

This trip was discouraging for Alexander. It seemed that his problems would never end. His good friend Hephaestion got sick and died, and Alexander felt deep sorrow. He also missed his horse, Bucephalus. Alexander was badly hurt, too. He continued traveling and fighting for about eight months, but his body would not get better. Some **historians** think he may have caught **malaria** from an insect bite. Alexander became very ill. He died in Babylon on June 13, 323 B.C.E., at age 33. He never returned to his homeland.

Combining two cultures

Alexander wanted the Greeks and Persians in his **empire** to get along. He mixed the two groups as much as possible. Alexander gave Persians and Greeks important positions in the government and in the army. He encouraged his men to choose Persian wives. One day, he held a large group wedding. Alexander and more than 80 of his men married Persian women. Alexander also got married that day to his second wife, Darius's daughter Stateira.

After Alexander

After Alexander's death, his **empire** started to fall apart. Without Alexander to keep control, many problems arose throughout the region.

New leadership

When Alexander died, both of his wives were pregnant. Roxane had Stateira killed so that her own child could rule. Roxane's son, Alexander, shared power with his uncle, Philip Arrhidaeus. But the boy was too young to lead well, and Philip Arrhidaeus was a weak ruler. Other people who wanted power killed both rulers and Roxane. However, no one was able to hold power for long.

The life of Alexander

Although Alexander the Great ruled for only about thirteen years, he is remembered as one of the greatest leaders of all time. His army traveled more than 22,000 miles (35,400 kilometers) through the **Middle East** and Asia. Alexander's soldiers defeated some of the most powerful people—and some of the most dangerous new weapons—in that part of the world.

▲ The Alexander sarcophagus was thought to have been made for Alexander after he died. It was really built for a king from a city called Sidon. A sarcophagus is a fancy stone coffin.

Alexander tried to help the different people in his empire live together. Sometimes, he chose to treat the people he conquered with kindness instead of killing them or making them slaves. However, he and his soldiers unfortunately did kill thousands of people as well. As a result, people have different opinions of how Alexander should be remembered in history.

Alexander did try to combine the Persian and Greek ways of life. He tried to help people share ideas, knowledge, and ways of doing things. This sharing affected their development in art, science, government, language, and other areas. Alexander also **founded** many cities that still exist, such as Alexandria in Egypt. His travels helped open trade **routes** through his empire. For all of his successes, many people think he truly deserves to be called Alexander the Great.

▼ **This picture of Alexander was carved in wood by a German artist in the 1800s.**

Glossary

adviser person who gives help or advice

archaeologist person who finds out about the past by studying the remains of buildings and other objects

armor special clothing or covering worn to protect the body

artifact object that was made or used by humans in the past

cavalry soldiers on horseback

chariot light cart with two wheels that is pulled by horses

city-state independent city and its surrounding territories that has its own ruler

custom usual way of doing something

found to start something, such as a city or school

empire large land or group of lands ruled by one person or government

general leader of an army

historian person who studies and writes about the past

infantry soldiers who fight on foot

literature writings such as stories and poems

malaria illness causing fever and chills that is usually spread by mosquitoes

Middle East lands between the Mediterranean Sea and India

oasis green area in the middle of a desert where plants can grow

oracle holy place where Greeks went to consult a god or goddess about their future

orator person who is skilled in making speeches in public

pharaoh ruler of Egypt

philosopher thinker who tries to understand the world, the purpose of the universe, and the nature of human life. The word is Greek for "someone who loves knowledge."

port place on the coast or on a large river where ships load and unload

revolt uprising by people against their rulers

route path or way to get somewhere

strait narrow channel of water connecting two larger bodies of water

surrender to give up power to another person or group

temple building in which people worship a god or gods

tomb burial place, often marked by a stone or building

tribe group of people who share common ancestors, homeland, and way of life

tutor person hired to teach a child at home

Time Line

359 B.C.E.	Philip II becomes king of Macedonia
356 B.C.E.	Birth of Alexander
342 B.C.E.	Aristotle becomes Alexander's **tutor**
340 B.C.E.	Alexander joins the Macedonian army
338 B.C.E.	Alexander fights his first battle, at Chaeronea
336 B.C.E.	Philip II is killed; Alexander becomes king of Macedonia
333 B.C.E.	Alexander defeats Darius III and the Persians at Issus
332 B.C.E.	Alexander visits Egypt and is named **pharaoh**; founds city of Alexandria
331 B.C.E.	Alexander defeats Darius at Gaugamela
330 B.C.E.	Darius is killed; Alexander becomes Great King of Persia
326 B.C.E.	Alexander defeats Porus; Bucephalus dies
323 B.C.E.	Death of Alexander the Great

Pronunciation Guide

Word	You say
Achilles	a-KILL-eez
Aristotle	AIR-ih-STOT-ull
Bucephalus	byoo-SEFF-a-lus
Chaeronea	CARE-uh-NEE-ah
Darius	duh-RYE-us
Demosthenes	dih-MAHSS-theh-neez
Gaugamela	GAW-guh-MEE-lah
Granicus	gruh-NIGH-kus
Hephaestion	hih-FESS-tee-ahn
Isocrates	eye-SOCK-ra-teez
Leonidas	lee-ON-ih-dus
Macedonia	MASS-ih-DOE-nee-uh
Olympias	oh-LIM-pee-us
Persepolis	pur-SEP-uh-liss
proskynesis	PRAHS-ki-NEE-sis

More Books to Read

Langley, Andrew. *Alexander the Great*. New York: Oxford University Press, 1998.

MacDonald, Fiona. *Alexander the Great*. Broomall, Pa.: Chelsea House, 2000.

Taylor, Pat. *The Ancient Greeks*. Chicago: Heinemann Library, 1998.

Williams, Brian. *Aristotle*. Chicago: Heinemann Library, 2002.

Index

J   Pancella, Peggy.
B
Alexande Alexander the Great.
r
P

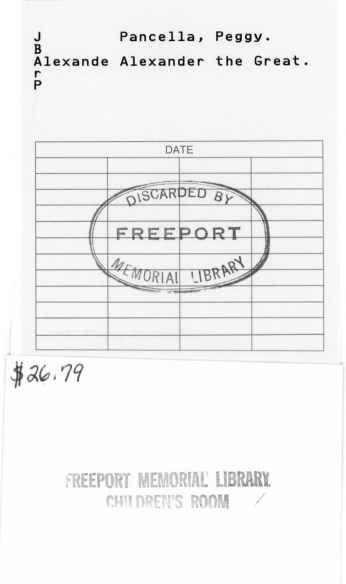